Ripley's

Believe It or Not!

# TIME WARP

The past and present collide!

**PUBLISHING**

Executive Vice President, Intellect
Senior Director of Publishing   Am;
Editorial Director   Carrie Bolin
Editor   Jessica Firpi
Designer   Mary Eakin
Researcher   James Proud
Proofreader   Rachel Paul
Fact checker   Jordie R. Orlando
Reprographics   *POST LLC

Penguin
Random House
UK

For more information regarding permission,
contact:

VP Intellectual Property
Ripley Entertainment Inc.
7576 Kingspointe Parkway
Suite 188
Orlando, Florida 32819
Email: publishing@ripleys.com
www.ripleys.com/books

A CIP catalogue record for this book is
available from the British Library.

Printed in China

PUBLISHER'S NOTE
While every effort has been made to verify
the accuracy of the entries in this book, the
Publisher cannot be held responsible for any
errors contained in the work. They would be
glad to receive any information from readers.

WARNING
Some of the stunts and activities are
undertaken by experts and should not be
attempted by anyone without adequate
training and supervision.

# Ripley's Believe It or Not!

# TIME WARP

The past and present collide!

RIPLEY
PUBLISHING

a Jim Pattison Company

A light bulb at a fire department in California has been operational since

# 1901—

the year Australia became a country.

Beijing, China,

had existed for $300$ years by the time Ancient Rome was founded.

# Woolly mammoths
### existed for centuries after the
## Egyptian pyramids were built.

Charles Darwin and
Abraham Lincoln
were born on the same day—February 12,

1809.

The fax machine was patented

# five days

after the first major wagon train
set off down the Oregon Trail in

## 1843.

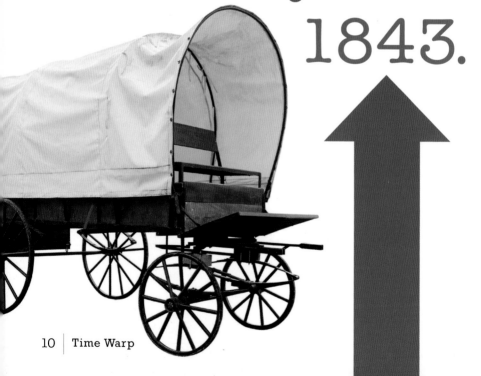

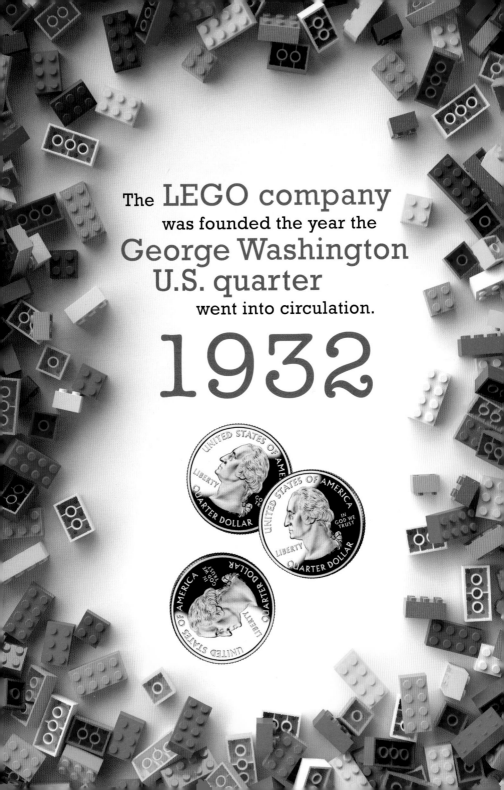

The LEGO company
was founded the year the
George Washington
U.S. quarter
went into circulation.

1932

# The Samurai
### fought their last battle the year of the first

# Wimbledon tennis championship.

THE CHAMPIONSHIPS WIMBLEDON

1877

Abolitionist and spy
# Harriet Tubman's life
## (1822–1913)
overlapped with former presidents
# Thomas Jefferson
# and Richard Nixon.

The book *I, Robot* was published in

# 1950,

the same year

Disney's *Cinderella* was released.

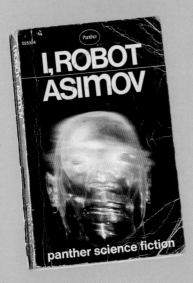

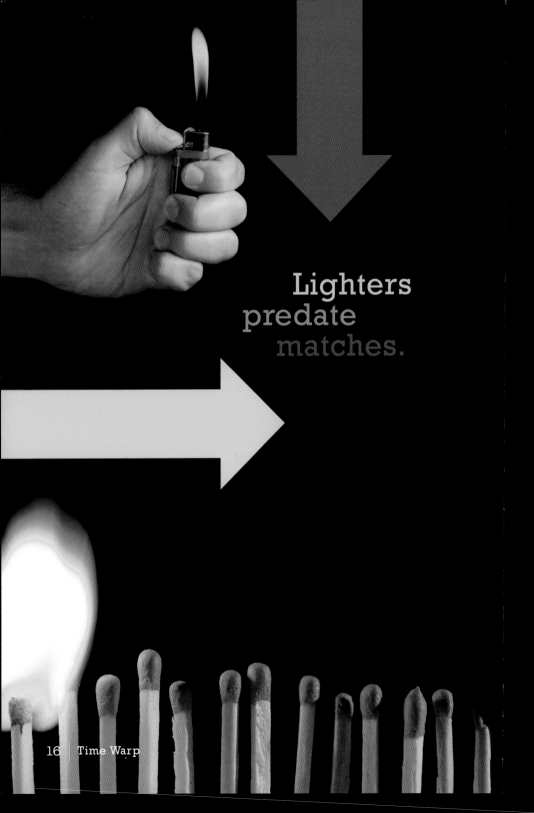

Lighters predate matches.

**Samuel Seymour** of Maryland witnessed the **assassination of Abraham Lincoln** and talked about it on television in **1956.**

# Grand Central station

has been around

# 54 years

longer than the Aztec Empire.

GRAND
TERM

The first email
was sent during
the Vietnam War, in
1971.

Between when we discovered Pluto (1930) and declassified it as a planet (2006), Pluto still has not completed an orbit around the sun.

Jupiter

Mars

Earth

Venus

Mercury

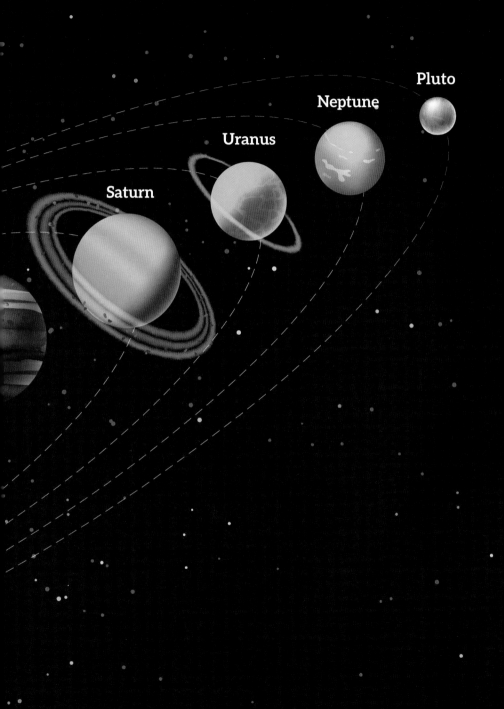

Saturn

Uranus

Neptune

Pluto

The first contact lenses were created in

# 1887.

The Russians safely landed a spacecraft on the Moon for the first time the same year that *Star Trek* premiered.

**Beauvais Cathedral** in France is still unfinished, despite construction starting at the time of the **Crusades,** almost

800

years ago!

A **clam** discovered in

# 2006

is thought to have been alive
at the same time as

## Christopher Columbus.

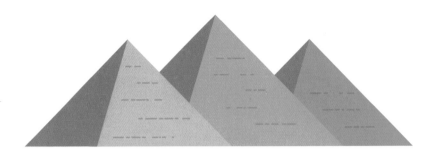

The Great Pyramid of Giza was the tallest structure in the world for almost

# 4,000 years.

Fairy tale author
# Hans Christian Andersen
was alive during the American
# Civil War.

Telephone pioneer
# Alexander Graham Bell

and Thomas Edison

were born within a month of each other in

1847.

# Oreos were introduced the year...

the Republic of China

was established.

The painter Vincent Van Gogh was born one year before Louis Vuitton was founded in 1854.

The world's oldest living
land animal,
Jonathan the giant tortoise, has lived through

the last 39 of the 45
U.S. presidents.

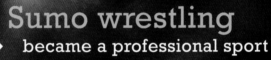

# Sumo wrestling
became a professional sport
in Japan around the same time...

Shakespeare's *Hamlet* was first performed.

The **Atlanta Braves**
were founded the year that
Germany became a country in

# 1871.

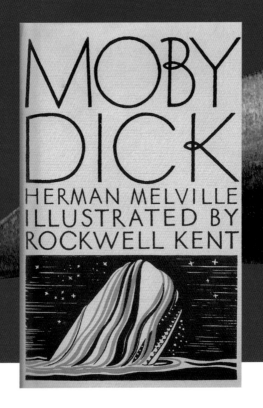

There are **whales**
alive today who were born before
**Herman Melville** wrote
*Moby Dick.*

The Eiffel Tower
opened the same year
Nintendo was founded as a
card company.

# Superman is older than World War II.

### He first appeared in

## June 1938.

**Louisiana** became a U.S. state **a few months** before **the waltz** was introduced in English ballrooms.

People were racing horses in the
**Kentucky Derby** for more than

# 20 years

before the first modern
**Olympic Games**
in Athens in

# 1896.

We made it to the Moon only

# 65 years after the Wright brothers invented human flight.

The last witchcraft trial
to take place in the United Kingdom was during
World War II, in

# 1944.

Sherlock Holmes
first appeared in print less than two months after
the elevator was patented in

# 1887.

The Himalayan Kingdom
of Bhutan finally allowed television in

1999!

When the Colgate toothpaste company was founded, Thomas Jefferson was president.

The Chinese invented toilet paper **100** years before Columbus landed in America.

Less than $40$ years separates the first microchip and Google.

The Moon landing and the TV debut of *Scooby-Doo, Where Are You!* both happened in

# 1969.

# Pocahontas was born in
# 1596,
one year before Shakespeare's
## *Romeo and Juliet*
was published.

THE
MOST EX=
cellent and lamentable
Tragedie, of Romeo
and *Iuliet*,

*Newly corrected, augmented, and
amended:*

As it hath bene sundry times publiquely acted, by the
right Honourable the Lord Chamberlaine
his Seruants.

LONDON
Printed by Thomas Creede, for Cuthbert Burby, and are to
be sold at his shop neare the Exchange.
1599.

The **passenger pigeon** went extinct the year World War I began.

Kim Kardashian
and Colonel Sanders
were alive at the same time.

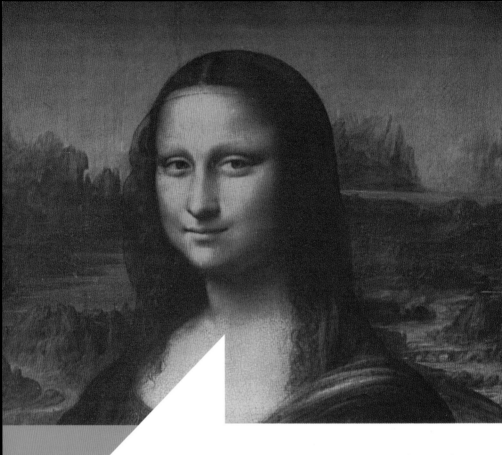

It took Leonardo Da Vinci up to **16** years to finish painting the **Mona Lisa...**

while it took
Michelangelo just 4 years
to paint the ceiling of the
Sistine Chapel.

The first Internet domain was registered the same year that *Back to the Future* premiered.

# 1985

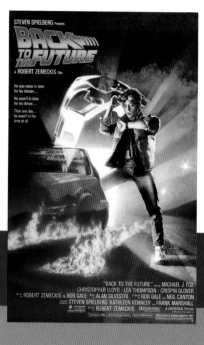

China had writing paper around

# 800 years

before it appeared in Europe.

105 A.D. vs. 900s A.D.

Jellyfish existed
# 350 million years
before dinosaurs.

The state of Mississippi did not officially
**abolish slavery** until February

# 2013.

- - - - - - - - - - - - - - - - - - - - - - - - - - - - - - - - - - - - - - - - - - - -

When the **Spanish** first made contact,
the **Inca Empire** numbered

# 12 million people,

more than the entire
Spanish empire at the time.

The **Converse All-Star basketball shoe** was introduced in

# 1917–

# 32 years

before the NBA existed.

**Shakespeare** was writing plays when the **Jamestown colony** was established in Virginia in **1607.**

Sewing needles, rope,

boats, and the flute were all invented

thousands

of years

before the wheel.

The Viking **Leif Erikson** landed in North America almost **500** years before **Columbus** did.

The fifth actor to portray James Bond,
Pierce Brosnan, is the same age as
James Bond——he was born
the year the first book was published.

*Star Wars* was released
May **1977...**

France's **last guillotine**
beheading took place less than
**4 months later.**

The **telephone**
was patented the same year
that **sardines** were first canned
in Maine.

American alligators
walked the Earth
at the same time as the
T. rex.

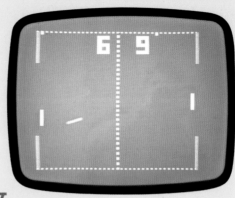

**Elvis Presley**
lived long enough to play
console computer games.

In **1971,**
it rained in an area of the
Atacama Desert, Chile,
for the first time in
**400** years.

# Pixar's *Toy Story 3*

### was released the same day the

# last execution by firing squad

### happened in the

# United States.

# Pablo Picasso, J. R. R. Tolkien, and Bruce Lee all died in...

## 1973.

The game of $bingo$ was introduced to North America the same year the Wall Street market crashed.

# 1929

STOCK MARKET CRASH AHEAD

The **oldest living tree** was growing when **Stonehenge** was being built—more than **5,000** years ago!

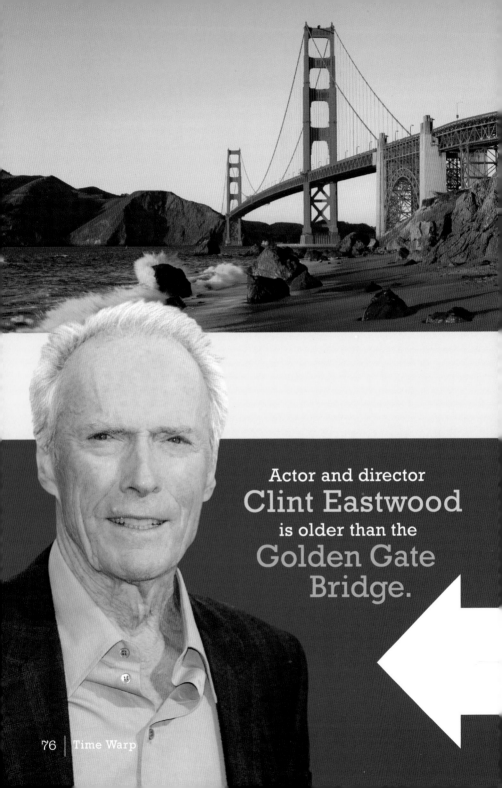

Actor and director
**Clint Eastwood**
is older than the
**Golden Gate
Bridge.**

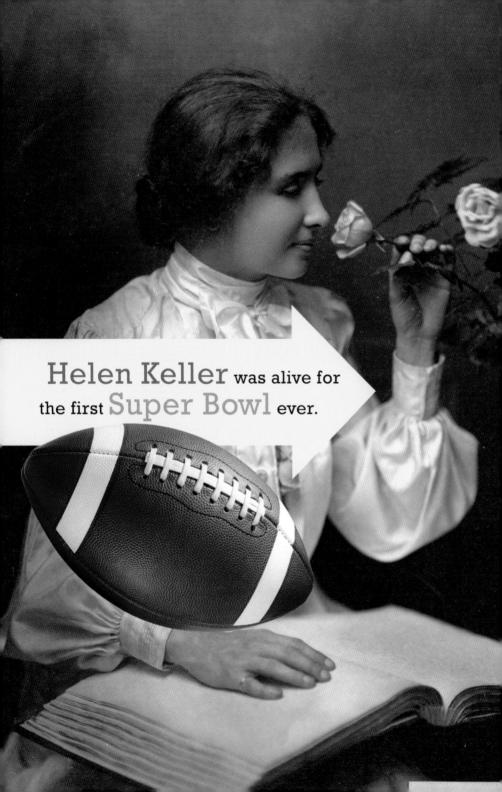

Helen Keller was alive for the first Super Bowl ever.

Thomas Jefferson's handwritten French fry recipe predates French fry cookbook recipes by half a century.

Sausages
are older than the
Bible.

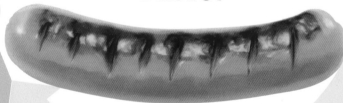

The **Canadians** started celebrating
Thanksgiving

# 42 years

before **the pilgrims**
arrived in America.

Silent movie star **Charlie Chaplin** lived long enough to see the release of the home PC in **1977.**

Canada became a country in

# 1867

but completed its independence
114 years later.

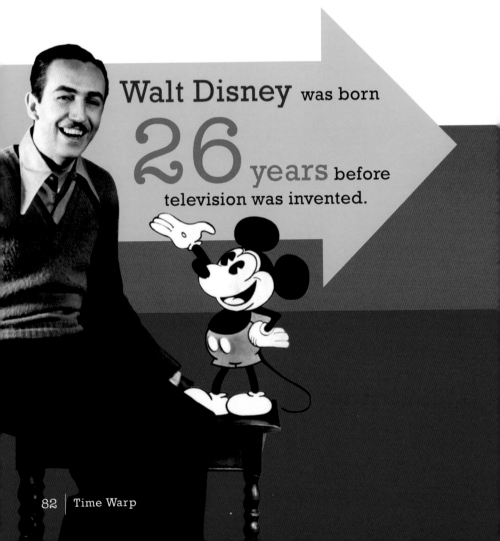

Walt Disney was born

## 26 years before

television was invented.

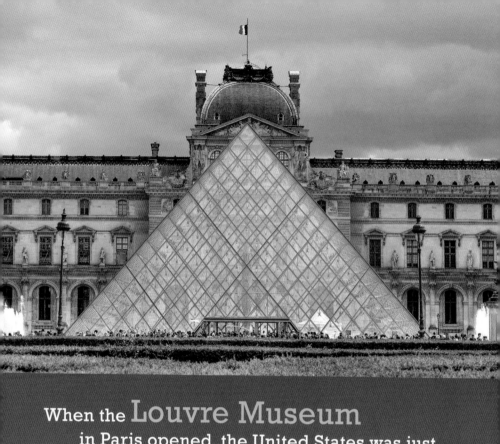

When the **Louvre Museum** in Paris opened, the United States was just

**17** years old.

The **Stegosaurus** and the T. rex never coexisted. They are separated by about

# 85 million years.

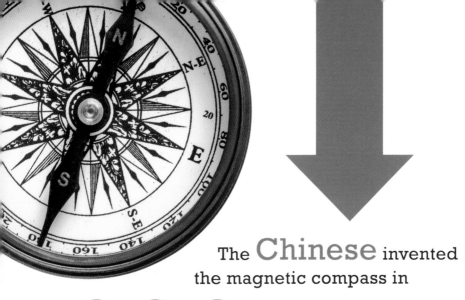

The **Chinese** invented
the magnetic compass in

# 206 B.C.,

during the Han Dynasty—more than

# 1,000 years

before compasses appeared in

## western Europe.

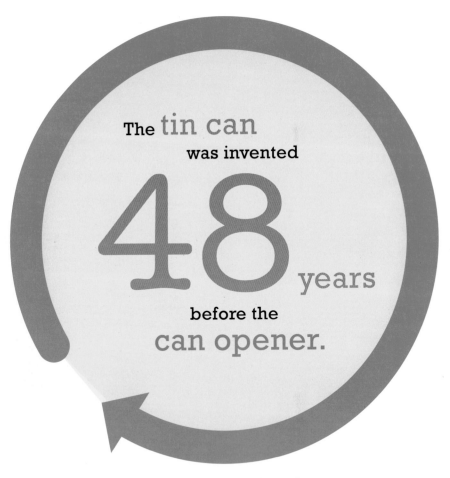

The tin can was invented

48 years

before the can opener.

1810/1858

The **first human to human blood transfusion** took place

# 151 years

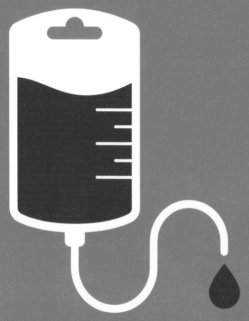

**after** the first animal to human transfusion.

## 1818 vs. 1667

The **steam train** predated the **bicycle** by **13** years!

The last surviving **American Civil War veteran** lived to see color television in

# 1953.

Cleopatra lived closer in time to the building of the **first Pizza Hut** than the building of the **Egyptian pyramids.**

Both **John Adams** and **Thomas Jefferson** died on July 4,

# 1826–

exactly **50 years** after the adoption of the **Declaration of Independence.**

In **1953**...
# Queen Elizabeth II
was crowned,
**DNA** was discovered,

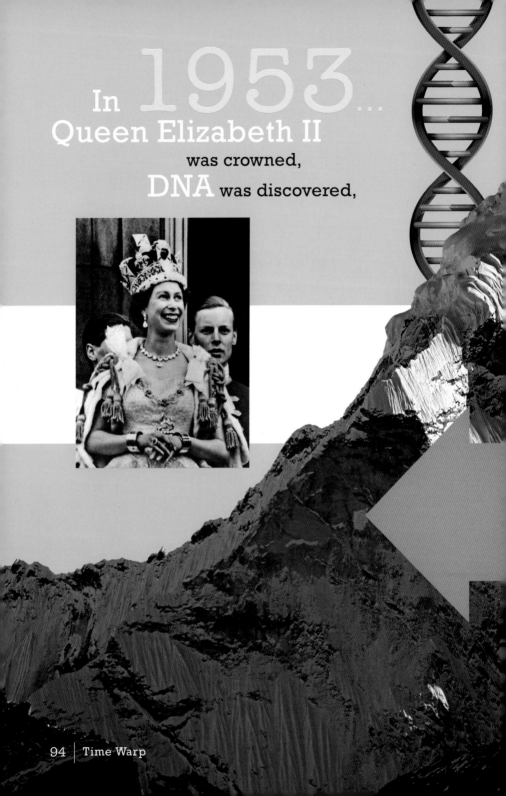

the first James Bond book was published,
and climbers reached the summit of
Mount Everest
for the first time.

Civil rights heroine **Rosa Parks**
lived long enough to watch

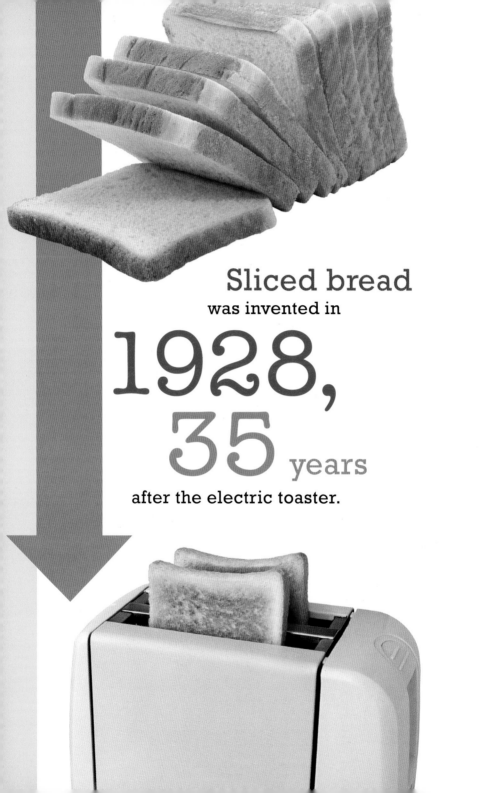

Sliced bread was invented in **1928,** **35** years after the electric toaster.

# Marilyn Monroe and Queen Elizabeth II

were born within three months of each other in...

1926.

The word "scientist" was not invented until

# 1834,

more than 100 years after the death of Sir Isaac Newton.

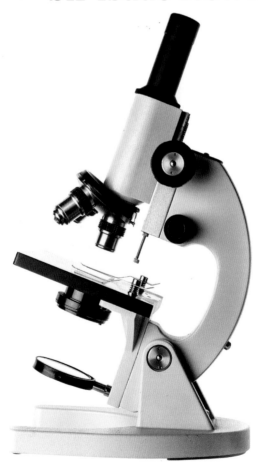

# Macy's department store was founded before Italy became a country.

- - - - - - - - - - - - - - - - - - - - - - - - - - - - - - - - - - - - - - - - -

The first-ever Porsche car, made in

# 1900,

was electric.

**"O.M.G."**
was first used in a letter to
**Winston Churchill**
during World War I, in 1917.

The first sighting of the
**Loch Ness monster** was in the year
**565.**

The
**second sighting**
of the mythical monster
was not for another
**1,368 years!**

ANNE FRANK

THE DIARY OF A YOUNG GIRL

WITH AN INTRODUCTION BY ELEANOR ROOSEVELT

Anne Frank
was born
the same year as
Martin Luther King Jr.
1929

The first known mechanical alarm clock was invented the same year the U.S. Constitution was created in 1787.

Every two minutes,
we take as many photos
as all of humanity took during the

1800s.

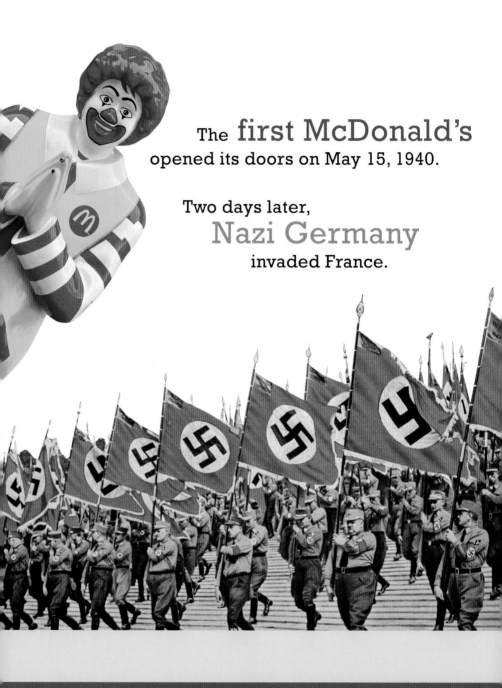

The **first McDonald's** opened its doors on May 15, 1940.

Two days later, **Nazi Germany** invaded France.

Soda was invented in **1767,** while Mozart was alive.

People have been saying "God bless you" after sneezes for more than

1,400 years!

The piano was invented less than **10** years after the Salem witch trials.

The modern smartphone has more computing power than all of NASA had when it put astronauts on the Moon.

# 1911

The computer company IBM was founded the **same year** the first explorer reached the South Pole.

-------------------------------------------------------

Beethoven was 20 when Mozart died in 1791.

**Mahatma Gandhi**
was assassinated the year
NASCAR
was founded—**1948.**

The first woman member of the U.S. Congress began her first term

before women had the right to vote.

1916/1920

There have been

# 426 more years

of gladiator competitions in Rome than years the

## United States

has been a country.

# Michael Jackson, Prince, and Madonna were all born in
# 1958.

The **car** was invented before the game of **basketball**.

Women were excluded from the
**Olympics track and field** until

# 1928,

the same year Amelia Earhart
flew across the Atlantic.

HAMMOND·Y

DEPARTMENT OF COMMER

BUREAU OF AIR COMMERCE

**Emilio Palma** of Argentina was the first person ever born in **Antarctica**—he only turns **40** in **2018!**

When *The Simpsons* first aired,

the Soviet Union still existed.

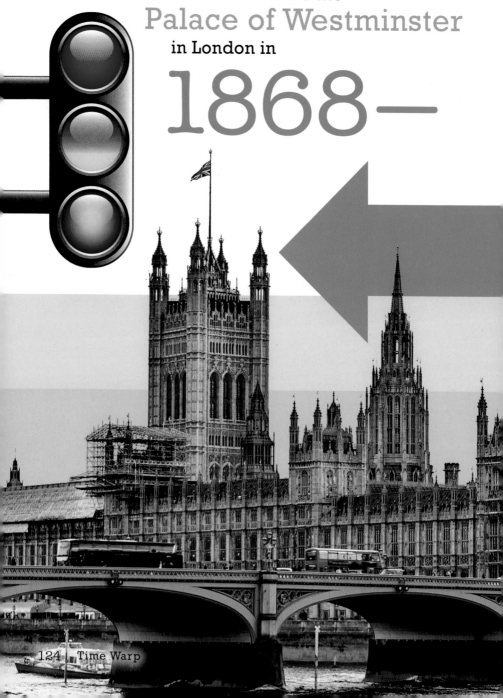

The **first traffic signals**
were installed outside the
Palace of Westminster
in London in

# 1868–

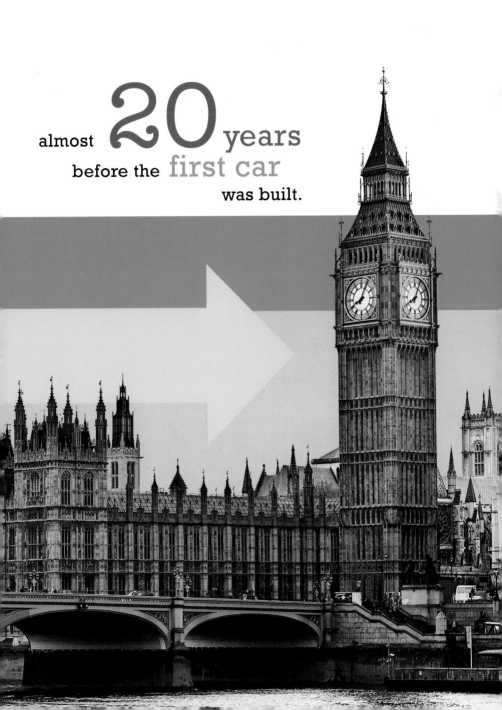

almost **20** years before the first car was built.

# Oxford University
is older than Spain—by almost

# 400
years!

1096/1469

The vacuum cleaner
was invented the same year
Abraham Lincoln
was elected president in

1860.

Sabre-tooth
tigers
were still around when humans
first began farming

11,000 years ago.

The **Beatles** released their first single in

# 1962, the same year

## Native Australians

got the right to vote
in federal elections.

The first **flushing toilet**
was invented during the time of
Shakespeare in

# 1596.

THERE IS
O DARKNESS
BUT
GNORANCE

# When New York City was founded, the dodo still existed.

# J. D. Salinger,

### author of *The Catcher in the Rye*,
### lived long enough to read
## books on a Kindle.

# Teddy Roosevelt
witnessed **Abraham Lincoln's** funeral procession in

# 1865.

---

# Mickey Mouse
debuted the same year
## clip-on ties
were designed.

# 1889

The jukebox
was invented the year
**Adolf Hitler**
was born.

There are Greenland sharks
alive today that are older than the
United States.

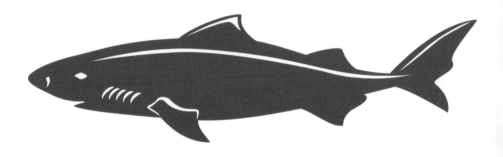

The first documented emoticons,

:-) and :-(

were posted on
Carnegie Mellon University
Bulletin Board System just five years after the first
color computer was released in 1977.

The first known use of the
@ symbol was in

# 1536–

the same year
Henry VIII executed
Anne Boleyn.

When Apple was founded in
# 1976,
Spain was still a dictatorship.

- - - - - - - - - - - - - - - - - - - - - - - - - - - - - - - - -

Confucius, Buddha,
and Pythagoras
were all alive at the same time in the

# 5th
century B.C.

The **Brooklyn Bridge** is older than

London's Tower Bridge by **11** years.

The last surviving widow of a
## U.S. Civil War veteran died in
# 2004!

---

The modern **sewing machine**
was invented five years before
the **safety pin.**

1844 vs. 1849

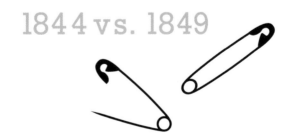

The current population of
New York City is greater than
that of Earth

# 10,000 years ago.

NEW YORK

LEONARDO DiCAPRIO     KATE WINSLET

NOTHING ON EARTH
COULD COME BETWEEN THEM.

A JAMES CAMERON FILM

# TITANIC

FROM THE DIRECTOR OF 'ALIENS', 'T2' AND 'TRUE L

The movie *Titanic* is **34 minutes longer** than it took the actual ship to sink.

# Acknowledgments

**Cover** Design by Mary Eakin; **14** (b) Alpha Historica/Alamy Stock Photo, (ct) North Wind Picture Archives/Alamy Stock Photo, (cb) Glasshouse Images/Alamy Stock Photo; **15** (l) Chris Howes/Wild Places Photography/Alamy Stock Photo, (r) Moviestore collection Ltd/Alamy Stock Photo; **23** Photo 12/Alamy Stock Photo; **26** (t) Sabena Jane Blackbird/Alamy Stock Photo; **27** (r) Moviestore collection Ltd/Alamy Stock Photo; **29** (t) CBW/Alamy Stock Photo; **30** Sueddeutsche Zeitung Photo/Alamy Stock Photo; **31** David Cole/Alamy Stock Photo; **34-35** Simon Benjamin/Alamy Stock Photo; **38-39** WILDLIFE GmbH/Alamy Stock Photo; **38** (c) Heritage Image Partnership Ltd/Alamy Stock Photo; **40** (l) Shady Lewis/Alamy Stock Photo; **41** (t) carlos cardetas/Alamy Stock Photo; **51** (b) WENN Ltd/Alamy Stock Photo; **52** (b) Moviestore collection Ltd/Alamy Stock Photo; **53** (l) Chronicle/Alamy Stock Photo, (r) Ian Dagnall/Alamy Stock Photo; **56** Chad Ehlers/Alamy Stock Photo; **58** The Advertising Archives/Alamy Stock Photo; **61** imageBROKER/Alamy Stock Photo; **63** (r) Lou-Foto/Alamy Stock Photo; **65** (l) Rod Collins/Alamy Stock Photo, (r) Collection Christophel/Alamy Stock Photo; **67** Enrique RAmos/Alamy Stock Photo; **69** (t) INTERFOTO/Alamy Stock Photo, (b) ScreenProd/Photononstop/Alamy Stock Photo; **71** Photo 12/Alamy Stock Photo; **72-73** (dp) ScreenProd/Photononstop/Alamy Stock Photo; **72** (bl) Guillem Lopez/Alamy Stock Photo, (br) ScotStock/Alamy Stock Photo; **76** (t) Sydney Alford/Alamy Stock Photo; **77** (bkg) Chronicle/Alamy Stock Photo; **81** (t) INTERFOTO/Alamy Stock Photo, (b) Photo 12/Alamy Stock Photo; **82** Ronald Grant Archive/Alamy Stock Photo; **94** (l) Pictorial Press Ltd/Alamy Stock Photo; **95** (t) AF archive/Alamy Stock Photo; **96** (b) World History Archive/Alamy Stock Photo; **98** Bettmann/Contributor via Getty Images; **99** Max Mumby/Indigo/Getty Images; **103** (t) CBW/Alamy Stock Photo, (b) Glasshouse Images/Alamy Stock Photo; **114** (r) Lebrecht Music and Arts Photo Library/Alamy Stock Photo; **118** (tl) sjvinyl/Alamy Stock Photo, (tr) AF archive/Alamy Stock Photo, (b) CBW/Alamy Stock Photo; **122** AF archive/Alamy Stock Photo; **128** (t) Marc Tielemans/Alamy Stock Photo; **132** (l) ZUMA Press, Inc./Alamy Stock Photo, (r) Martin Williams/Alamy Stock Photo; **133** (l) WALT DISNEY/Ronald Grant Archive/Alamy Stock Photo

**Key:** t = top, b = bottom, c = center, l = left, r = right, dp = double page, bkg = background

All other photos are from Shutterstock.com

Every attempt has been made to acknowledge correctly and contact copyright holders, and we apologize in advance for any unintentional errors or omissions, which will be corrected in future editions.

Stop by our website daily for new stories, photos, contests, and more!

## www.ripleys.com

  /RipleysBelieveItOrNot  @Ripleys

youtube.com/Ripleys  @RipleysBelieveItorNot